Text by Frederick C. Klein

For the Love of Baseball

An A-to-Z Primer for Baseball Fans of All Ages

Illustrations by Mark Anderson

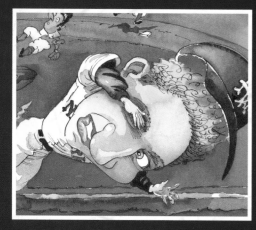

For nearly a century and a half baseball has been providing us with wonderful and enduring memories that are passed from generation to generation. The feats of the game's greatest players and the moments of high drama stand the test of time as parents share stories with their children, who in turn entertain their own children with memories of our great national pastime.

As a result of this time-honored tradition, I've had the good fortune to become a permanent fixture in baseball lore. My "Shot Heard 'Round the World," which won the 1951 National League pennant for the New York Giants, is a historic moment that has become an indelible memory, a story passed along to new generations of fans over the years. I am both humbled and privileged to hold such a place in the annals of baseball, and it thrills me to be able to play this small part in the history and tradition of our great game. *For the Love of Baseball* was created in the same spirit, with a wish to preserve memories, honor legends, and respect all that this game and its stars have given us. In words and pictures, its creators have captured the wonderful history and tradition of this uniquely American institution, and I am honored to be a part of it.

—**Bobby Thomson**

"A" is for Hank Aaron,

Who hit with great power.
His records, if piled,
Would top the Sears Tower.

HANK AARON was, statistically, baseball's greatest slugger, holding 12 major league career batting records when he retired in 1976. He set the mark for most home runs (755) and runs batted in (2,297) in his 23 seasons with the Milwaukee (and then Atlanta) Braves and the Milwaukee Brewers. After his playing days he became an executive with the Braves. Other notable players whose last names begin with A include Adrian "Cap" Anson of the Chicago Cubs, the best hitter of the pre-1900 era, and two shortstops with the Chicago White Sox, Luke Appling and Luis Aparicio. One of Appling's talents was for wearing out pitchers by endlessly hitting foul balls.

"B" is for Babe Ruth,

"The Sultan of Swat,"
"The Babe," "The Bambino,"
Who once called his shot.

GEORGE HERMAN "BABE" RUTH was, in the opinion of many, the greatest baseball player of all time. He began his major league career as a pitcher for the Boston Red Sox and excelled in that capacity, leading the Red Sox to the 1918 World Championship. Sold to the New York Yankees in 1920, he was switched to the outfield because of his hitting ability, and went on to set records for most home runs in a season (60 in 1927) and career home runs (714) that stood for many years. It is said that on October 1, 1932, in a World Series game against the Chicago Cubs, he pointed toward the center-field stands and proceeded to hit a home run to that same spot. Some people question whether Ruth really "called his shot," but the incident is part of baseball lore. The Babe's closest modern-day counterpart is Barry Bonds of the San Francisco Giants, whose 73 home runs in 2001 epitomized the game's recent power wave.

"C" is for Ty Cobb,

Who slid with spikes high.
Between the white lines
He'd never say die.

TY COBB was baseball's best hitter, averaging .366 over 24 seasons (1905–1928), all but two of which he spent with the Detroit Tigers. He was an uncompromising competitor who had few friends in the game, even among his own teammates, but his hit-to-all-fields batting style and slashing base running set enduring standards. Three other C stars were Latin Americans: **Orlando Cepeda** and **Roberto Clemente**, from Puerto Rico, and **Rod Carew**, from Panama. Cepeda hit with power for several National League teams during the fifties and sixties, while Clemente stood out at the plate and in right field for the Pittsburgh Pirates at about the same time. Carew was a left-handed placement hitter in the Cobb mold over 19 seasons (1967–1985) with the Minnesota Twins and the California Angels.

"D" is for Joe DiMaggio,

Whom all fans embrace—
The sleek "Yankee Clipper,"
Whose trademark was grace.

JOE DIMAGGIO was the New York Yankees' center fielder from 1936 through 1951, except during his three years of World War II service. A .325 lifetime hitter and holder of the consecutive-game hitting record (56, set in 1941), he was known almost equally for his powerful throwing arm and his skill and range in the field. One of his keenest competitors during much of his career was his younger brother, Dominic, who played center field for the Boston Red Sox, the Yankees' archrivals. Another brother pair was Arkansas-born pitchers **Paul** and Dizzy Dean, who starred for the 1934 World Series—winning St. Louis Cardinals. Dizzy Dean later became a baseball broadcaster who made fans smile by using such countrified words as *swang* and *slud*.

"E" is for Ernie Banks,
The "Let's Play Two" man.
He was tops in Cub homers,
And tops with the fans.

ERNIE BANKS played with the Chicago Cubs as a shortstop and first baseman from 1953 through 1971. He retired

as the team's career home-run leader, with 512. His cheerful disposition and love of the game made him the all-time

fan favorite of the venerable franchise. Second baseman Johnny Evers

was an earlier Cub hero who, with shortstop Joe Tinker and first baseman

Frank Chance, led the team's 1907 and 1908 world-champion clubs.

Thanks partly to a poem about them, Tinkers-to-Evers-to-Chance remains baseball's

most famous double-play combination.

"F" is for Bob Feller,

Who came off of the farm,
And mowed down the hitters
With his rapid right arm.

BOB FELLER, from Van Meter, Iowa, nicknamed "Rapid Robert," made his major league debut at age 18 with the

Cleveland Indians, becoming an instant star with a 17-strikeout game against the Philadelphia A's. He went on to win

266 games for the Indians, and led the American League in strikeouts seven times. Other great pitchers whose names started with F were Edward "Whitey" Ford, the best New York Yankees starter in the late fifties and early sixties, and Rollie Fingers, the ace reliever on the Oakland A's championship clubs of the seventies. Fingers' trademark was his wide, wax-tipped mustache.

"G" is for Lou Gehrig

Who knew only one way:
The great "Iron Horse"
Came to play every day.

LOU GEHRIG was the power-hitting first baseman of the champion New York Yankee teams of the twenties and thirties. He was a .340 lifetime hitter who drove in 100 or more runs for 13 straight seasons. His consecutive-game streak of 2,130 was a record for many years until it was broken by Baltimore Oriole Cal Ripken Jr. in 1995. The "G men" Hank Greenberg and Charlie Gehringer did their best to thwart Gehrig's teams while leading the Detroit Tigers to American League pennants in 1934, 1935, and 1940. The 6'4" Greenberg was a two-time AL Most Valuable Player who hit 58 home runs and drove in 183 runs in 1938. Gehringer was a slick-fielding second baseman who batted over .300 in 13 different seasons.

"H" is for Rogers Hornsby;
His vision was fine.
He battered the pitchers
Like rugs on a line.

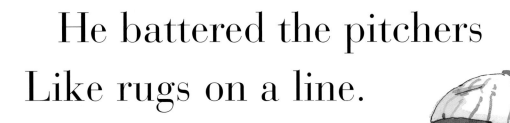

ROGERS HORNSBY, who played for 23 years with the St. Louis Cardinals, the Chicago Cubs, and other teams, had a lifetime batting average of .358, the highest ever for a right-handed hitter. In one season—1924—he hit .424. He was a great believer in physical fitness, and even refused to watch movies or read for fear of damaging his eyesight. Hornsby contemporaries **Harry Heilmann** and **Gabby Hartnett** also were handy with a bat. Heilmann had a .340 lifetime mark and won four American League batting titles with the Detroit Tigers in the twenties. Hartnett was a rugged catcher with the Chicago Cubs whose home run in near darkness against the Pittsburgh Pirates—the famous "Homer in the Gloaming"—clinched the 1938 pennant for his team.

"I" is for innings,

The standard is nine.
But if the game's tied,
Then more are just fine.

Whether it was the top of the first, the bottom of the ninth, or somewhere in between, Monty Irvin was a fearless hitter who had a brief but impressive major league career. He was one of several veteran players who made the jump from the Negro Leagues to the majors after baseball lifted its color barrier in 1947. He was a key contributor to the pennant-winning New York Giants teams of 1951 and 1954, batting .458 in the 1951 World Series.

"J" is for Walter Johnson,

The Senators' "Big Train."
For 21 seasons,
He caused hitters pain.

WALTER JOHNSON of the Washington Senators, nicknamed "The Big Train," ranks high on any list of baseball's greatest pitchers. A right-handed fastballer with a sweeping, sidearm delivery, he won 417 games from 1907 through 1927, and struck out 300 or more hitters in nine different seasons. His 110 career shutouts are still a record. **Ferguson Jenkins** was a latter-day righty with a knack for strikeouts. He played for the Chicago Cubs, the Texas Rangers, and the Boston Red Sox in the sixties and seventies, and was the first Canadian-born player elected to the Hall of Fame. **Reggie Jackson** made his living tormenting pitchers—and other foes—with long home runs. His World Series exploits with the Oakland A's and the New York Yankees in the seventies and eighties earned him the nickname "Mr. October."

"K" is for Sandy Koufax,

A lefty with verve.

His fastball was unhittable,

And so was his curve.

SANDY KOUFAX'S career was cut short by an elbow injury, but for six seasons—1961 through 1966—he dominated

the game as few pitchers have. He won 129 times for the Los Angeles Dodgers in that stretch, including four no-hitters,

and led the National League in earned run average five times. His ERA in his four World Series was 0.95. Los Angeles'

opponent in the 1965 Series was the Minnesota Twins, led by slugging third baseman Harmon Killebrew.

When he retired in 1975, his 573 home runs ranked second only to Babe Ruth's 714 among American Leaguers.

Unfortunately for "Killer" and the Twins, Koufax and the Dodgers won the '65 Series in seven games.

"L" is for Judge Landis,

With gusto he gaveled.
If it weren't for him,
Baseball might have unraveled.

KENESAW MOUNTAIN LANDIS was the federal judge whom the Major League Baseball team owners named as their first commissioner. He was appointed in 1920, after baseball was shaken by the revelation that eight Chicago White Sox players had conspired to allow the Cincinnati Reds to win the 1919 World Series. Landis often ignored the rules of evidence and sometimes handed down arbitrary decisions, but he is credited with helping restore public confidence in the game during his 24-year tenure.

"M" is for Willie Mays,

Leo's "Say Hey!" kid.
His catch on Vic Wertz
Stopped the Indians' bid.

WILLIE MAYS joined manager Leo Durocher's New York Giants in 1951 as a bubbly 20-year-old whose signature line was "Say Hey!" He went on to have one of baseball's most remarkable careers. He hit with power over 22 seasons, as his 660 home runs attest, but shone equally in the field and on the base paths. The tape of his over-the-shoulder catch of a drive by the Cleveland Indians' Vic Wertz in the 1954 World Series is probably baseball's most replayed highlight. Stan "The Man" Musial of the St. Louis Cardinals and Mickey Mantle of the New York Yankees were two other all-time greats. Musial sprang from his coiled, left-handed stance to win seven National League batting titles in the forties and fifties. The switch-hitting Mantle led the championship Yankee teams of the fifties and sixties.

"N" is for Phil Niekro,

Whose pitches went fluttering.
He sent many a batter
Back to the bench muttering.

PHIL NIEKRO, a longtime Atlanta Brave, was a leading exponent of the knuckleball, a slowly delivered pitch that has little or no spin and dances in the air currents around home plate. While the pitch can be hard to hit, it's also hard to control and catch, so knuckleballers are rare. Niekro was an exception, winning 318 games in a 24-season career that ended in 1987. Another notable knuckleballer was **Hoyt Wilhelm**, a reliever who appeared in more than 1,000 games and played with nine different teams in the fifties and sixties.

"O" is for outs,

Which come in several ways:
On the ground, in the air,
Or in breeze-stirring "K's."

Some baseball "O's" were anything but zeroes. Mel Ott was a smallish man, standing 5'9" and weighing about 170 pounds, but he hit 511 home runs in a career with the New York Giants that began in 1926, when he was 17 years old, and ended 22 years later. The left-hander had an odd swing that began with his front (right) leg cocked high. After his playing days, he managed the Giants and later joined their front office staff.

"P" is for Satchel Paige,

Whose large bag of tricks
Kept him pitching till 60,
Still getting his kicks.

LEROY "SATCHEL" PAIGE was a Negro Leagues star who was said to have mastered more than a dozen different pitches. He didn't get the opportunity to play in the majors until 1948, when he was 42 years old. After five seasons there, he played for a dozen more years in the minor leagues and with touring teams before finally retiring just short of his 60th birthday. Still, since the birth date he used was widely questioned, he might have been several years older. A number of Negro Leaguers who were among the best players of their eras never had the chance to perform in the majors. They included catcher and power hitter Josh Gibson, legendary base stealer James "Cool Papa" Bell, and Cuban-born pitcher Martin Dihigo, Paige's frequent rival on the mound.

"Q" is for the question:

Who's the greatest, all-time best?
There's really no answer,
So you can't flunk the test.

"R" is for Jackie Robinson,

Who broke the color ban.
Few players have shone brighter,
As an athlete, or a man.

In 1947, Jackie Robinson became major league baseball's first African-American player. He went on to play for 10 seasons with the Brooklyn Dodgers, a span in which the team won six National League pennants. Robinson's role as a racial pioneer made him the target of jibes from opposing players and fans. Instead of responding verbally, he played with an aggressive style epitomized by his 19 steals of home. In 1997, Major League Baseball retired his uniform number, 42, for all of its teams. No other player has been so honored. Two other unrelated Robinsons—Brooks and Frank—teamed up memorably with the champion Baltimore Orioles teams of 1966 and 1970. Brooks Robinson was a career Oriole known especially for his prowess at third base. Frank Robinson was an outfielder who hit 586 home runs in 21 seasons, mainly with the O's and the Cincinnati Reds. He later became a major league manager and a league and team executive.

"S" is for Casey Stengel;

The lineups he'd juggle.

His teams won 10 pennants

Without too much struggle.

CHARLES DILLON "CASEY" STENGEL had the most remarkable run of any baseball manager, winning 10 American

League pennants and seven World Series titles in his 12 seasons with the New York Yankees (1949–1960). He also

amused and confused fans with his imaginative use of the English language. The Hall of Fame's manager list also

includes John McGraw, the longtime New York Giants skipper (1902–1932), and **Walter Alston** and **Tommy

Lasorda** of the latter-day Los Angeles Dodgers.

"T" is for Bobby Thomson,

Whose "Shot Heard 'Round the World"
Left Brooklyn's banners wrapped,
While the Giants' were unfurled.

BOBBY THOMSON was a journeyman outfielder who played for five major league teams over his career. His claim to fame is hitting what was probably the most famous home run in baseball history. That came on October 3, 1951, at New York's Polo Grounds, in the ninth inning of the deciding game of a National League playoff between his New York Giants and the Brooklyn Dodgers. It gave the Giants a come-from-behind, 5–4 victory, and the NL pennant. The three-run blow was dubbed "The Shot Heard 'Round the World." An earlier Giant who made a mark on the game was **Bill Terry**. The soft-spoken Georgian had a career batting average of .341 over 14 campaigns, excelled at first base, and later managed the team.

"U" is for the umpires,
Klem, Hubbard, and all.
No one's out or safe
Until they make the call.

Early baseball umpires were subject to considerable harassment which sometimes caused them to shade their judgments in order to avoid such persecution. **Bill Klem**, who umpired in the major leagues for 36 years (1905–1940), is credited with creating the posture of unbending decisiveness that became the profession's standard. He's in the Hall of Fame as an ump, along with **Cal Hubbard**, who, as a younger man, earned National Football League star status as a lineman for the New York Giants and the Green Bay Packers.

"V" is for ultimate victory,

Each team's holy grail.
But, alas, every season,
All but one has to fail.

"W" is for Ted Williams,

Whose picture-perfect swing
Made Fenway fans cheer
When his home runs took wing.

TED WILLIAMS lived to hit a baseball, and did it very well. Over 19 seasons, the career Boston Red Sox left fielder combined superb physical coordination with a scientific approach to batting to achieve a .344 average and smash 521 home runs. His .406 average in 1941 was the last time a major leaguer hit .400 or better. After he retired, the onetime "Splendid Splinter" wrote a classic book on how players should swing a bat and think about the strike zone. Honus Wagner, who was anything but picture-perfect, was the best player of the first two decades of the 20th century. Thick-chested, bowlegged, and ungainly looking, the Pittsburgh Pirate nonetheless hit for a .328 average over 21 seasons (1897–1917), and starred at shortstop as well.

"X" marks the ballot
Of every future name
Like Sosa, Johnson,
and Maddux
Who'll be in the Hall of Fame.

Sammy Sosa of the Chicago Cubs, a native of the Dominican Republic, hit 60 or more home runs in three seasons (1998, 1999, and 2001), something no other player had done at the time. Left-handed pitcher Randy Johnson, who stands 6'11", blazed a strikeout trail with the Seattle Mariners and the Arizona Diamondbacks, and led the D'Backs' 2001 championship run. Right-handed pitcher Greg Maddux was almost a foot shorter than Johnson. He relied on deception and control to win 15 or more games in 16 straight seasons with the Cubs and the Atlanta Braves, who won National League pennants in 1995, 1996, and 1999.

"Y" is for Denton "Cy" Young.

His win total is why
The awards for best pitcher
Are nicknamed "The Cy."

CY (FOR "CYCLONE") YOUNG was a right-handed pitcher with 511 victories over a 22-season career (1890–1911, spent mostly with the Cleveland Indians and the Boston Red Sox)—a record that isn't likely to be broken. A big man and a hard thrower, he played during an era when starting pitchers commonly threw 40 or more complete games in a season, and thus had high win (and loss) totals. His performance stood out nonetheless, and when Major League Baseball created its best-pitcher awards for each league in 1956, it named them for him. **Carl Yastrzemski**, another ex–Red Sox player, bashed pitchers heartily during his long (1961–1983) career with the team. In 1967, he became the last man to win a Triple Crown for league-highest batting average (.326), most home runs (44), and most runs batted in (121).

"Z"

...is the sound

Someone makes when he snoozes.

A baseball fan stays loyal

Even when his team loses.

"**A**" is for Hank **Aaron**

"**A**" is for "Cap" **Anson**

"**B**" is for **Babe** Ruth

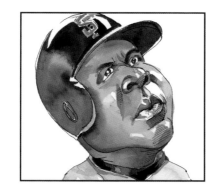

"**B**" is for Barry **Bonds**

"**C**" is for Ty **Cobb**

"**C**" is for Roberto **Clemente**

"**D**" is for Joe **DiMaggio**

"**D**" is for Dizzy **Dean**

"**E**" is for Ernie **Banks**

"**E**" is for Johnny **Evers**

"**F**" is for Bob **Feller**

"**F**" is for "Whitey" **Ford**

"**G**" is for Lou **Gehrig**

"**G**" is for Hank **Greenberg**

"**H**" is for Rogers **Hornsby**

"**J**" is for Walter **Johnson**

"J" is for Reggie **Jackson**

"K" is for Sandy **Koufax**

"L" is for Kenesaw Mountain **Landis**

"M" is for Willie **Mays**

"M" is for Mickey **Mantle**

"N" is for Phil **Niekro**

"P" is for Satchel **Paige**

"R" is for Jackie **Robinson**

"R" is for Frank **Robinson**

"R" is for Brook **Robinson**

"S" is for Casey **Stengel**

"T" is for Bobby **Thomson**

"U" is for **Umpire**

"W" is for Ted **Williams**

"W" is for Honus **Wagner**

"Y" is for Cy **Young**